# STRAIGHT UP
# SELLING

## YOUR TOOLBOX FOR
## SALES EXCELLENCE

Includes 35+
Downloadable
Worksheets

010001101          110        11
10010000001110        1
100100110001011        1
001110100011001010111100

# MORT GREENBERG

# OTHER BOOKS
# BY <u>MORT GREENBERG</u>

## THE SINGULAR FOCUS
100+ Tips to Maximize Your Revenue

## REVENUE BOOST
The Ultimate Sales Plan in Five Steps

# What Others Are Saying ...

**Tim Horan** | Chief Growth Officer, Pattern Health

Working directly with Mort I have seen first hand the consistent and predictable results his sales system delivers. Mort has always treated selling as a science, so if you are serious about elevating and optimizing you or your organization's performance, these are must read books for you.

"

**Joe Britton** | Founder & CEO SearchMarketers

Straight Up Selling is a MUST have for your entire sales team. So many books are too high level making it difficult to learn where to start or how to execute. Straight Up Selling provides you with clear and concise tools and tactical steps to crush your sales goals. Not only have I used this method when working in big corporations, but also applied these exact tools to build my company to the #4 Fastest Growing Company in America - Deloitte. There are MILLIONS of dollars worth of secrets to fast track your sales success in this book!

"

**Jim Diaz** | Former VP / SVP, Sales Excite, Ask Jeeves, Turn

Mort and our teams scaled multiple digital sales driven companies from millions to hundreds of millions of dollars in annual revenues over the course of a decade. He was instrumental in innovating the transformation from purely relationship driven, transactional selling to automated sales through platforms driven by real time analytics. Mort has an innate ability to thread the needle between humans and machines, creating sales strategies that sustain success over time.

"

**Brian Berger** | Founder and CEO Mack Weldon
(Former Sales Colleague at Excite@Home)

Mort's straightforward and relatable style is relevant for most sales situations. As colleagues, he always made our clients feel like was their advocate which was key in earning their trust. This was authentic and real – no BS.

**Alex Boyce** | COO / CBO Dash Radio/DXSH.MV

Mort was not only technically one of my first 'bosses,' but a friend, mentor and someone I credit with helping shape my career. Mort's focus on the difference between 'revenue' and 'sales' changed my perception of our objectives as sales leaders and was critical in my professional progression.

**Jonathan Sandak** | Founder WooHooMarketing and Account Executive, NBCUniversal

Mort focuses on helping sellers achieve their best. Four times over the years I have been on teams with Mort: IAC, Nokia, iHeartMedia, and Sunset Magazine. At each company we relied on the same systems in this book to plan our go to market strategy and scale our revenue. This book is as close as you can get to working with him 50+ hours per week.

**Douglas Neiman** | Founder & CEO Navio Networks

Mort is not only an experienced seller, but has always been an amazing listener to what clients need. He then leverages these two skills, coupled with incredible organizational talents, to create a system that continues to prove successful for all sellers who have worked for him.

# STRAIGHT
## UP SELLING

Your Toolbox for
Sales Excellence

digitalCORE
PUBLISHING

DIGITALCORE PUBLISHING

Copyright © 2022 by

Mort Greenberg

Cover design and illustrations by Asiel

First Paperback edition December 2022

ISBN: 979-8-9873618-8-7 (eBook)

ISBN: 979-8-9873618-7-0 (Print)

Published by digitalCORE, Inc.

http://dgtlcore.com/

FOR THOSE WHO DEMAND
MORE OF THEMSELVES THAN
OTHERS DO OF THEM

# REVENUE.
# MINDSET.

# AUTHOR'S NOTE

## Selling Can be Like Art

There is no question, like you, I love selling. Each day presents unique challenges and like a blank canvas you can fill it in as the right inspiration comes to you. For 25+ years, coming up with new solutions for customers is part of my joy of selling, hopefully, you feel the same.

Over the years I have written down various hacks and tips to help me continually improve as a seller and sales manager. Along the way, these nuggets became training segments that were tested over and over with hundreds of salespeople at companies, small and large.

Many of these items have been organized into the book that you are now holding and represent a straight-up way of selling. No gimmicks, just practical ways to improve your sales process.

There is a huge amount of thanks to give. To the sales managers that I worked for that showed me the way, to sellers that I was fortunate enough to work with and help along their way. And of course, thanks to our customers who made it all possible.

## Always Challenge Yourself

My comment to everyone, even if you are a first-day junior seller, is to challenge me. Never take my word for anything if you do not believe it. Test the idea, if it does not work, let me know and together we will improve.

So, with that concept of always challenging front and center, at the end of the book, there is a QR code to scan to provide a review or feedback. If you think there is a way that this book can be better, please let me know. Or if there are any items that you have tried from these pages and found do not work, let me know that as well. And... If you have any compliments, well, feel free to share those as well!

Since no one wants to just read about ideas without being able to quickly test them, there are a few worksheets in this book that you can start using from day 1.

In fact, on the following pages, there are 35+ worksheets available with this book. By scanning the QR code at the bottom of this note you can access all of them. Just add to the cart, for a no charge / free checkout.

Whether you take some elements from this book and combine them with your current systems or just use the systems laid out here, you will find a way to improve your sales process and overall revenue generation.

## Revenue vs. Sales

A key topic woven into this book is the difference between revenue and sales. Revenue is the outcome and end goal of selling. Where sales is the process we go through to generate revenue.

## Always Build Upon Your Skills

There are six types of sales training companies can utilize for their sellers: Industry Training, Company Training, Product Training, General Sales Training, Leadership Training, and Sales Technique Training. What you will read on the

pages ahead falls mainly into the last group, Sales Technique Training.

Learning how to sell is a never-ending process. Everyone in every aspect of life sells at one time or another. Anyone that has been a seller, even if a new seller, knows firsthand that success in sales does not come easily. It requires hard work, dedication, and a willingness to continually learn and improve.

That's why you put in the time and effort to become better at selling. Whether you're just starting out in your career or you're a seasoned pro, there is always room to improve. Two of the biggest drivers that push sellers to get better and better are customer expectations and personal satisfaction.

**Customer Expectations:** : Today's customers expect more from salespeople than ever before. They want knowledgeable, professional, and helpful salespeople who can provide them with valuable insights and solutions.

**Personal Satisfaction:** As a salesperson, there is nothing quite like the feeling of closing a sale and knowing that you've helped someone solve a problem or meet a need. By putting in the time and effort to become a better seller, you'll be able to experience success more often.

So, if you're serious about your career in sales, don't let complacency set in. Instead, commit to continuous learning, this will help you be the best seller possible. Your customers (and your bottom line) will thank you.

# Curriculum – 12 Sections

## BOOK INCLUDES COMPANION EXCEL WORKBOOKS

SECTION

**01.**

INTRODUCTION

- **OBJECTIVE:** [WHAT TO ACCOMPLISH]
  Develop Your Revenue Mindset
- **MISSION:** [PURPOSE]
  Improve Your Business Outcomes

SECTION

**02.**

Scaling Outreach to Beat Your Revenue Goals

SECTION

**05.**

Put in the time BEFORE, DURING & AFTER Meeting

SECTION

**06.**

The "NINE TOOL" to Inform Your Sales Process

SECTION

**09.**

"SEVEN STEP PR" to Gain Inbound Leads & Drive Revenue

SECTION

**10.**

Personal & Team Development Tools

SECTION

# 03.

How to Find the Best Prospects and Stand Out

SECTION

# 04.

Sales Writing & Employing Empathy

SECTION

# 07.

Forging Exceptionalism

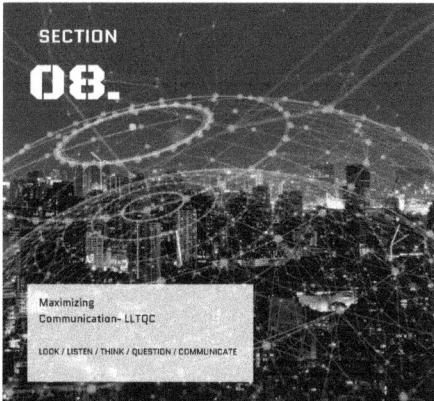

SECTION

# 08.

Maximizing Communication- LLTQC

LOOK / LISTEN / THINK / QUESTION / COMMUNICATE

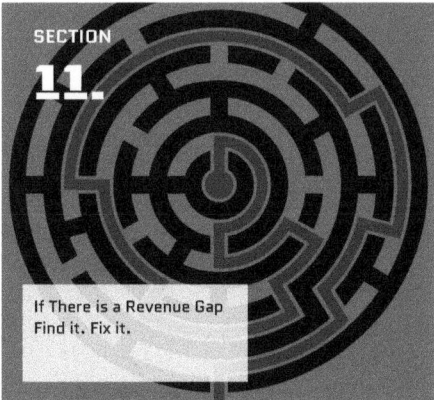

SECTION

# 11.

If There is a Revenue Gap Find it. Fix it.

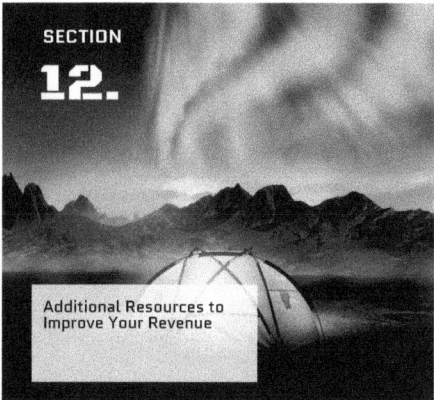

SECTION

# 12.

Additional Resources to Improve Your Revenue

# TABLE OF CONTENTS

## SECTION 5: Put In The Time Before, During & After Meetings .......................61

## SECTION 6: "The Nine Tool" To Inform Your Sales Process .......................78

## SECTION 10: Personal & Team Development Tools

## SEECTION 11: If there is a revenue gap Find it. Fix it

# Three Benefits of This Book

## 01.

Access New Tools To Grow Your Revenue Mindset

## 02.

Evolve Your Sales Process To Prioritize Prospecting & Follow-up

## 03.

Integrate Relentless Preparation Into Your Routine

# SECTION
# 01.

# INTRODUCTION

- **OBJECTIVE:** [WHAT TO ACCOMPLISH]
  **Develop Your Revenue Mindset**

- **MISSION:** [PURPOSE]
  **Improve Your Business Outcomes**

# REVENUE VS. SALES

$

## REVENUE IS NOT THE
## SAME AS SALES:

1. Revenue is the outcome of having a great sales process

2. Sales on its own takes time and is seen as a mystery to many who do not study sales

# THIS BOOK WILL
# ALLOW YOU TO:

1. Explore tools to grow your # of customers & new revenue

2. Create your own processes to bring more value to your customers

# Book Content For Anyone, But Mostly...

## B:B SALES

### (GOOD TIPS FOR B:C SALES TOO)

SELLERS

SALES MANAGERS

MARKETERS

BRAND MANAGERS

PRODUCT MANAGERS

BUSINESS DEVELOPERS

BUSINESS INVESTORS

SENIOR TEAMS

COMPANY OWNERS

# Setting Up Your Sales Process

• Sales is a Process, Revenue is the Reward

• 6 Month Units of Time

- **Unit 1**
Write & validate sales plan
→ months 1-6

- **Unit 2**
Improve plan and type of deals sold
→ months 7 - 12

- **Unit 3**
Drive revenue, Repeat Business, Scale
→ months 13 – 18+

**18 Months in Total to Hit Stride,**

**But Sell from Day 1**

# 02.

## Scaling Outreach to Beat Your Revenue Goals

# TASK #1 – Fold A Sheet Of Paper Into Six Boxes

| | | |
|---|---|---|
| **LIST YOUR TOP CLIENT**<br><br>(THINK ABOUT WHAT THEY LIKE MOST ABOUT YOUR DEAL) | **LIST YOUR TOP PROSPECT**<br><br>(THINK WHY THEY WANT TO BUY FROM YOU) | THIS BOX WILL BE FILLED IN LATER IN THE BOOK |
| **LIST 1 INDUSTRY ORG**<br><br>(YOU BELONG TO OR KNOW ABOUT AND SHOULD JOIN) | **THINK ABOUT A MENTOR**<br><br>(WHO IS SOMEONE THAT CAN BE A MENTOR TO YOU?) | THIS BOX WILL BE FILLED IN LATER IN THE BOOK |

# Know Your Goals to Beat Your Goals

## (Individual or Team)

- **Quarterly Tracking vs. Previous Year**

  - Goal v. actual by quarter for the year
  - Know the clients that helped you deliver last year

- **Weekly Walk to See "Outlook to Finish"**

  - Goal v. actual + pipeline for the current quarter
  - Always know where your quarter will finish
  - If there will be a shortfall ring the alarm bell early

# Quarterly Tracking vs. Previous Year

[YOUR LOGO HERE]

## YOUR COMPANY NAME          *202X CURRENT OUTLOOK*

*Data Source: Boostr reports*

CONFIDENTIAL. PLEASE DO NOT SHARE, FORWARD OR USE OUTSIDE OF YOUR TEAM.

|  | Q1 | Q2 | Q3 | Q4 | 20XX YTD |
|---|---|---|---|---|---|
| **20XX (000)** | | | | | |
| Quarter | Q1 | Q2 | Q3 | Q4 | 20XX YTD |
| Sales Goal | $ 4,000 | $ 4,500 | $ 5,000 | $ 6,500 | $ 20,000 |
| Contracted Current Week | $ 3,786 | $ 4,671 | $ 4,800 | $ 7,230 | $ 20,487 |
| Variance to Goal | $ (214) | $ 171 | $ (200) | $ 730 | $ 487 |
| % to Goal | 94.7% | 103.8% | 96.0% | 111.2% | 102.4% |
| | | | | | |
| Contracted Previous Week | $ 3,786 | $ 4,671 | $ 4,800 | $ 6,600 | $ 19,857 |
| **Variance vs. Previous Wk.** | $ - | $ - | $ - | $ 630.0 | $ 630.0 |
| | | | | | |
| Pipeline | $ - | $ - | $ - | $ 2,310 | $ 2,310 |
| End of QTR Projected Finish | $ 3,786 | $ 4,671 | $ 4,800 | $ 9,540 | $ 22,797 |
| % to Goal @ Projected Finish | 94.7% | 103.8% | 96.0% | 146.8% | 114.0% |
| | | | | | |
| **Year Prior Finish / Quarter** | $ 3,400 | $ 3,750 | $ 3,821 | $ 4,663 | $ 15,634 |
| $ Variance to Current Week | $ 386 | $ 921 | $ 979 | $ 2,567 | $ 4,853 |
| **% Variance to Current Wk.** | **11.4%** | **24.6%** | **25.6%** | **55.1%** | **31.0%** |

## BOOKED v. GOAL
### WEEKLY BOOKED BUSINESS TARGET = $XX

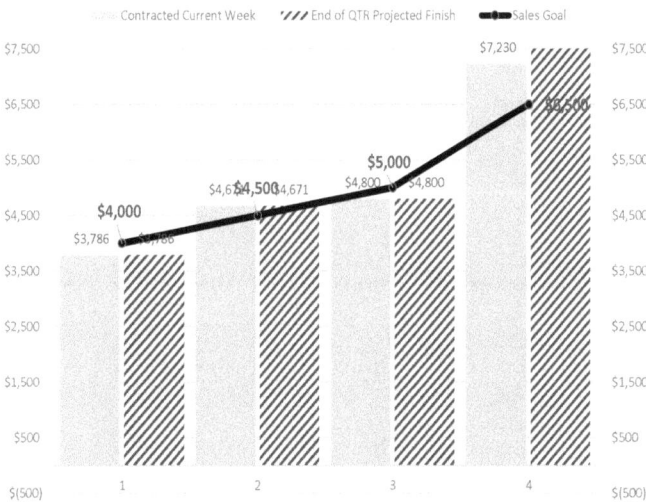

Legend: Contracted Current Week | End of QTR Projected Finish | Sales Goal

| | |
|---|---|
| $7,500 | $7,500 |
| $6,500 | $6,500 |
| $5,500 | $5,500 |
| $4,500 | $4,500 |
| $3,500 | $3,500 |
| $2,500 | $2,500 |
| $1,500 | $1,500 |
| $500 | $500 |
| $(500) | $(500) |

Data labels: $4,000 | $3,786 | $4,671 | $4,500 | $4,671 | $5,000 | $4,800 | $4,800 | $7,230 | $6,500

X-axis: 1   2   3   4

**NOTES**

Incudes $50k +/- per month of programmatic. Does not include subscriptions, or corp licensing revenue

Focus on New Business
5 / 5 / 30

# Weekly Update to Track Outlook to Quarterly Finish

[YOUR LOGO HERE]

CONFIDENTIAL. PLEASE DO NOT SHARE, FORWARD OR USE OUTSIDE OF YOUR TEAM.

| QX 202X (000) | | 1 | 2 | 3 | 4 | 5 | 6 | |
|---|---|---|---|---|---|---|---|---|
| | Week Of >>> | | | | | | | |
| Week Starting | | 4-Jul | 11-Jul | 18-Jul | 25-Jul | 1-Aug | 8-Aug | |
| Sales Goal | $ | 5,000 $ | 5,000 $ | 5,000 $ | 5,000 $ | 5,000 $ | 5,000 $ | |
| Contracted | $ | 2,449 $ | 3,122 $ | 3,400 $ | 3,550 $ | 3,600 $ | 3,812 $ | |
| Variance to Goal | $ | (2,551) $ | (1,878) $ | (1,600) $ | (1,450) $ | (1,400) $ | (1,188) $ | |
| % to Goal | | 49.0% | 62.4% | 68.0% | 71.0% | 72.0% | 76.2% | |
| W/W $Change (New Rev.) | $ | - $ | 673.00 $ | 278.00 $ | 150.00 $ | 50.00 $ | 212.00 $ | |
| Pipe $ to Convert Each Wk. | $ | - $ | - $ | - $ | - $ | - $ | - $ | |
| End of Wk. Projected Finish | $ | 2,449 $ | 3,122 $ | 3,400 $ | 3,550 $ | 3,600 $ | 3,812 $ | |
| % to Goal @ Projected Finish | | 49.0% | 62.4% | 68.0% | 71.0% | 72.0% | 76.2% | |

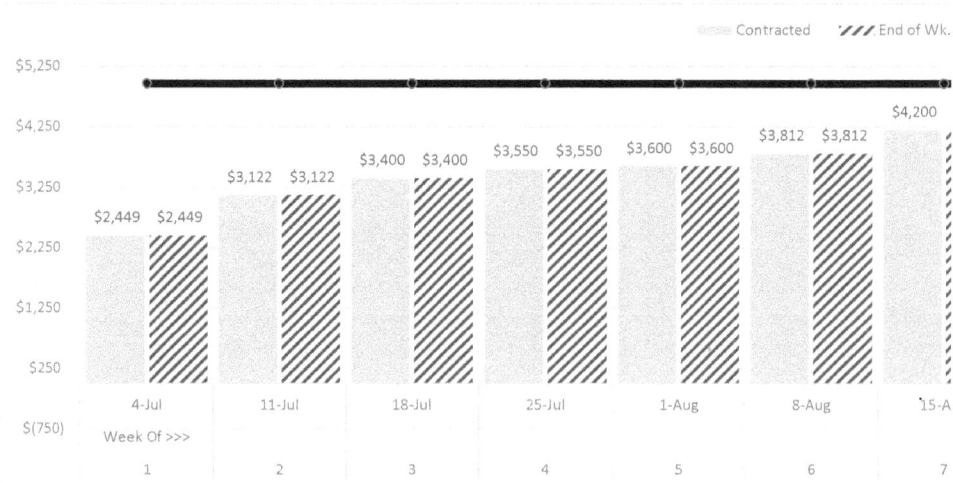

Contracted    End of Wk.

$5,250

$4,250                                                                                        $4,200

$3,250                                           $3,400 $3,400   $3,550 $3,550   $3,600 $3,600   $3,812 $3,812

$2,250           $3,122 $3,122

          $2,449 $2,449

$1,250

$250

$(750)

| | 4-Jul | 11-Jul | 18-Jul | 25-Jul | 1-Aug | 8-Aug | 15-A |
| Week Of >>> | 1 | 2 | 3 | 4 | 5 | 6 | 7 |

## OUTLOOK TO FINISH
### *WEEKLY BOOKED BUSINESS TARGET = $X*

| | 7 | 8 | 9 | 10 | 11 | 12 | 13 | NET $ in Q | Weekly Avg. |
|---|---|---|---|---|---|---|---|---|---|
| | 15-Aug | 22-Aug | 29-Aug | 5-Sep | 12-Sep | 19-Sep | 26-Sep | | ( 000 ) |
| $ | 5,000 | $ 5,000 | $ 5,000 | $ 5,000 | $ 5,000 | $ 5,000 | $ 5,000 | | |
| $ | 4,200 | $ 4,622 | $ 4,800 | $ 4,800 | $ 4,800 | $ 4,800 | $ 4,800 | | |
| $ | (800) | $ (378 | $ (200) | $ (200) | $ (200) | $ (200) | $ (200) | | |
| | 84.0% | 92.4% | 96.0% | 96.0% | 96.0% | 96.0% | 96.0% | | |
| $ | 388.00 | $ 422.00 | $ 178.00 | $ - | $ - | $ - | $ - | $ 2,351.00 | $ 195.92 |
| $ | - | $ - | $ 150 | $ 150 | $ - | $ - | $ - | | |
| $ | 4,200 | $ 4,200 | $ 4,950 | $ 5,100 | $ 5,100 | $ 5,100 | $ 5,100 | | |
| | 84.0% | 84.0% | 99.0% | 102.0% | 102.0% | 102.0% | 102.0% | | |

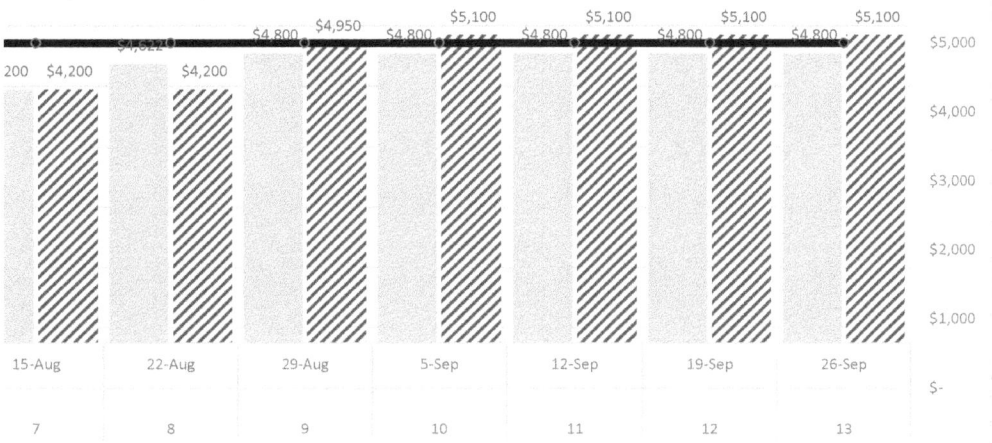

of Wk. Projected Finish — Sales Goal

# Scale Meeting Volume to Scale Revenue

• Everyone wants Zooms or in-person meetings

• But... Potential customers are overloaded

• Persistence helps you stand out

- 3+ emails and calls before a response back

- And remember... It is all about the follow-up

- Most people give up after the first follow-up

- Don't Give up! Just do not quit! That is the key

• Research your customers

- Find the latest news, press releases, stories, etc.

- Reference what you have learned in your follow-up

- Free time? Research customers. Learn all that you can

# Minimum Daily Activity – The 5's

- 5+ outbound (Emails / LinkedIn / Calls)

- 5+ follow-ups (Emails / LinkedIn / Calls)

- By end of the week, you now have 50+ people you engaged with.

*** Initially, rely on your effort, not on your network to get the meeting, but once you have put in the work to engage a prospect, then ask for help as it is needed***

## Let's Talk About "5"

- It is achievable

- It will create good habits

- It will help you beat your goals

## Minimum Daily Activity – The 5's

MUST EARN FOOD

**5+ OUTBOUNDS BEFORE LUNCH**

**5+ FOLLOW-UPS BEFORE DINNER**

# Key Items to Scale Outreach

- 5 Prospects for Immediate Outreach

- 50 Targets to Turn into Prospects

- 500 Contacts to Turn into Targets

- But where do you find leads?

- Let's talk about that...

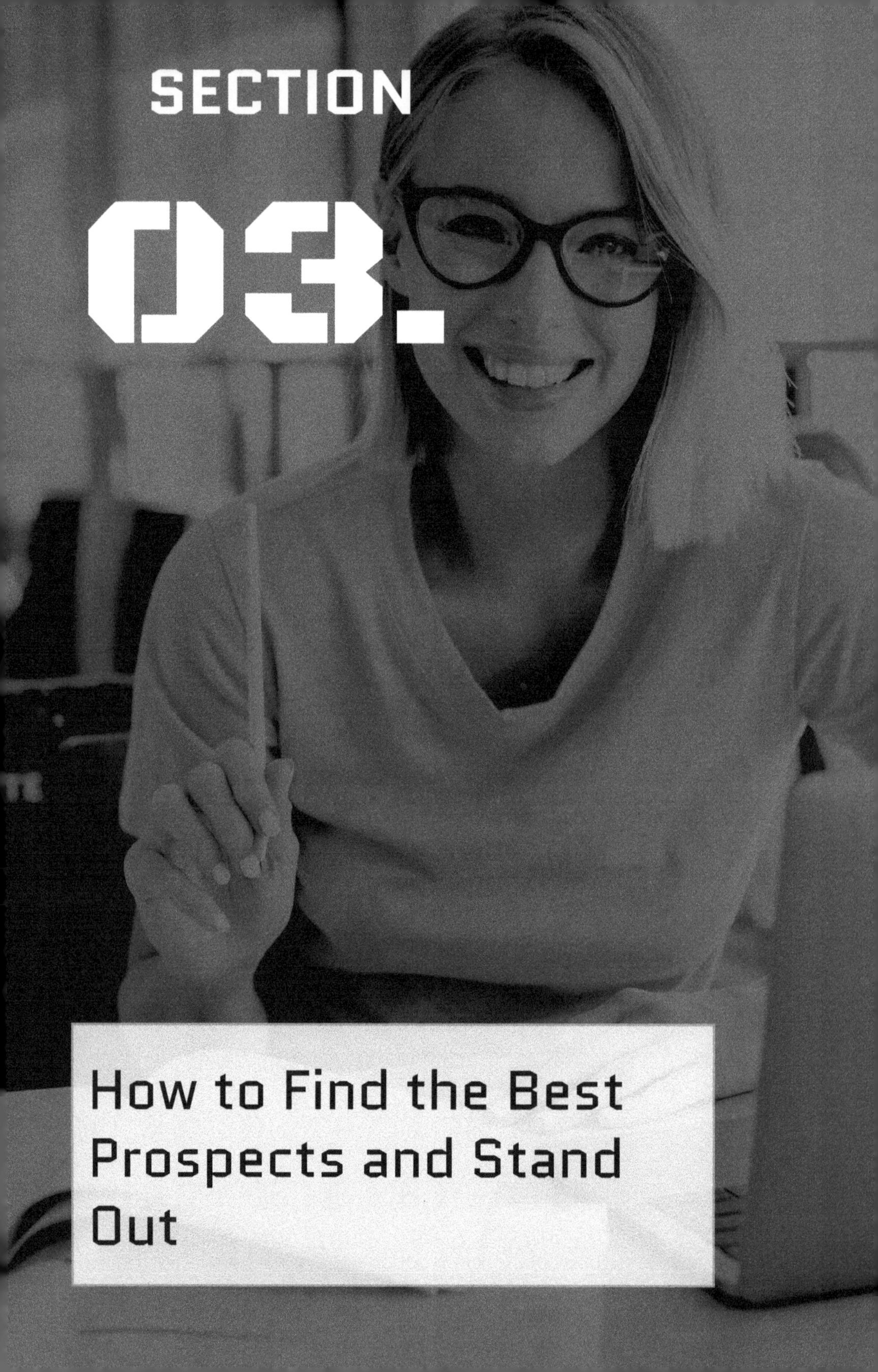

SECTION

# 03.

## How to Find the Best Prospects and Stand Out

# Prospecting Tips for B:B and B:C Sellers

- **For B:B Sales**

- Find Top Events / Conferences for Your Industry

- Copy List of All Sponsors & Exhibitors

- Note Which Are Customers, and Which Are Not

- Use ZoomInfo or Similar to Get Contacts at Non-Customer Co's

- Prioritize Each Non-Customer: A, B and C's

- **For B:C Sales**

- Content Marketing / Social to Drive List Sign Up

- Targeted Marketing Where Your Customers Spend Time

# Plan Your Prospecting Ahead of Time

- **Each Sunday Build Your Plan**

- Prioritize 25 co's you will engage each week, 5+ / day

- 25 / week = 100+ / month and 300+ / quarter

- With 300+ HIGH-quality prospects, you will always beat your #!

- **Each Morning Do Your Research**

- Each morning find 2 contacts at each of the 5 companies you will engage

- Google each person, find out something about them or their company

- Send a short, personalized email, earn a spot in their inbox

- **Each Afternoon Complete Follow-Ups**

- Follow up from emails sent the same day a week ago...

# Finding Your Best Prospects

- • List out top conferences and events in your industry

- - List both speakers & moderators

- • Read trade publications, make lists of prospects

- • Use Google, Hunter, Winmo, SellerCrowd, and

  ZoomInfo to get email addresses

- • Reach out and ask for a call or meeting

- - Ask to bring in lunch or send an UberEats card, etc

- - Create unique to you touches to build a relationship

- - A handwritten note or send a bottle of wine...

# Account Based Marketing (ABM)

- Account-based marketing (ABM) is when marketing and sales collaborate

- The collaboration creates personalized buying experiences for  high-value accounts

- Data-driven prospecting helps to ensure you identify the right accounts...

## FOUR KEY STEPS:

- **Identify:** Prioritizing high-value accounts

- **Expand:** Leverage content marketing and education emails regularly so you are not always directly emailing.

- **Engage:** Personalizing campaigns by platform (LinkedIn, Twitter, etc..) and content to address the unique needs of each target account

- **Advocate:** Align sales and marketing activities so prospects navigate the entire sales funnel and leave comments on social or reply to emails

# Test Selling Tools – CRM, ABM, Email Look Up & More...

**CRM**

| | |
|---|---|
| PROSPERWORKS | PIPEDRIVE |
| BOOSTR | HUBSPOT |

**CUSTOMER JOURNEY**

| | |
|---|---|
| YESWARE | PERSIST IQ |
| MARKETO | OUTREACH |

**LEADS & EMAIL LOOKUP**

| | |
|---|---|
| ZOOMINFO | HUNTER.IO |
| ROCKETREACH | LINKEDIN SLS. NAV. |
| MIGHTY SIGNAL | |

SALESFORCE

**ABM**

MADISON LOGIC

DEMANDBASE

TERMINUS

6SENSE

WINMO

INFOGROUP

DATA.AI

## Minimum Daily Activity – The 5's

**5+ OUTBOUNDS BEFORE LUNCH**

**5+ FOLLOW-UPS BEFORE DINNER**

- CHALLENGE YOURSELF – SHORTEST EMAILS EVERY TIME

- **Bullet #1 (Empathy)**
  - Check positive current company or personal news and congratulate
  - Or a reminder of your last interaction / how you \ met

- **Bullet #2 (Value)**
  - Who you are and what you do
  - How they can benefit by working with you

- **Bullet #3 (Goal)**
  - What do you want from them?

- **Bullet #4+ Additional info as needed**

- **Have pre-written Templates, But Customize Every Email by Recipient**

- **Never just blast out emails from a seller. You can blast out from marketing, product, or other non-seller**

## Sales Writing & Employing Empathy

# TASK #2 – Boost Your Visibility!

| LIST YOUR TOP CLIENT | LIST YOUR TOP PROSPECT | SOCIAL MEDIA ACCOUNTS |
|---|---|---|
| (THINK ABOUT WHAT THEY LIKE MOST ABOUT YOUR DEAL) | (THINK WHY THEY WANT TO BUY FROM YOU) | (DO YOU POST REGULARLY OR JUST A VOYEUR?) |
| LIST 1 INDUSTRY ORG | THINK ABOUT A MENTOR | IMPORTANT TREND TO YOU |
| (YOU BELONG TO OR KNOW ABOUT AND SHOULD JOIN) | (WHO IS SOMEONE THAT CAN BE A MENTOR TO YOU?) | (START POSTING AND REPOSTING ON THAT TOPIC) |

# Social Media – Become a "Smart" Content Creator

## Why & What to Post?

• Let people learn about you

• Motivate & educate

• When in doubt, take the conservative route

• Make your presence authentic to who you are as a professional seller

## When Posting...

• Check your spelling & grammar

• Create or share content with depth and a positive viewpoint

• Don't weigh in on politics

• Use great images/videos

• Post frequently

# Sales Writing – Maximize "You" and "Your". Rarely Use "I"

## Quality of Content

- The key to sales writing is empathy

- Focus on the person you are writing to

- Make a note about them, not you

- Never start a sentence, ever, with "I"

- Further, challenge yourself to never include "I" in any note or email

- Use our, we, and think through what you are trying to say

- Success is how many times the words you and your are included

# Quantity of Thought

- **Write in bullet points**

- No email with more than 5 bullets

- When angry keep to 3 bullets

- **Less content means you must think**

- Reduce words, condense goals, asks, etc.

- **Take time to write**

- You will save other's time and effort to understand your note and have less ?'s

- Makes it easier for them to know what is needed to help you

# Construction of Great Sales Notes

**12 OR LESS WORDS IN A SENTENCE**

**BE SPECIFIC**

**USE #'S & DATA WHEN YOU CAN**

**SPELL OUT ACRONYMS**

**AVOID YOUR INDUSTRY'S JARGON**

**ATTACH A CASE STUDY OR ONE SHEET**

# Phone Skills – Phone as the Perfect Follow-Up Tool

- Email first

- Email a second time

- Then call

- Earn a spot in their mind. No surprises, they know what you want, it is ok to ask!

*"If you call me directly without any prior notification, even without such as a simple text, in my mind you are one step removed from a telemarketer"* Found on LinkedIn from former Head of Starcom MediaVest

# SECTION

# 05.

Put in the time BEFORE, DURING & AFTER Meeting

# Create an Agenda with Your Customer

**People**

- List of attendees

**Meeting Goals**

- 2-3 goals for your time together

**Agenda Items**

- 5-8 items to cover in the meeting

**Notes**

- Always be the best note taker in the room

# MEETING AGENDA

| Meeting Leader | Date & Time of Meeting |
|---|---|
| **\<Enter Info\>** | **\<Enter Info\>** |
| Company/Division Meeting With | Meeting Location/Address or Zoom Link |
| **\<Enter Info\>** | \<Enter Info\> |

| < Enter Client Name> Attendees | \<Enter Your Company Name> Attendees |
|---|---|
| \<Enter Names> (Use ALT + Enter to add additional row(s)) | \<Enter Names> (Use ALT + Enter to add additional row(s)) |

**Meeting Goals**

1) Goal #1
2) Goal #2

**Meeting Agenda Items**

1) Item 1 (Use ALT + Enter to add additional row(s))
2) Item 2
3) Item 3
4) Item 4
5) Item 5

**Meeting Notes...**

# Share Customer Brief: Prep for People You Meet With

**Client Overview**

1. Short overview of customer business

**Situation Analysis**

1. What is going on in the customer's marketplace?

2. What are the competitor's customers thinking about?

3. What are the customer's major calendar events?

4. What is putting pressure on customers biz right now?

**Needs Assumption**

1. Current Understanding of Objectives and Strategies

2. Unique business Practices

**C U S T O M E R** BRIEF

*Date Prepared:*   **[date]**        *Customer:*      **[client name]**

**1. Client Overview**

**2. Situation Analysis**
*A. What is going on in the customer's marketplace*

*B. Who are the cor*

*C. What are the cu*

*D. What is putting*

**C U S T O M E R** BRIEF

*Date Prepared:*   **[date]**        *Customer:*      **[client name]**

**1. Client Overview**

**2. Situation Analysis**
*A. What is going on in the customer's marketplace*

*B. Who are the competitors and competitive product offerings the customer is thinking about?*

*C. What are the customer's major calendar events or impending product or marketing dates?*

*D. What is putting pressure on the customers business right now?*

# Share Customer History: Prep for People You Meet With

## Account Overview

1. How long have you worked with the customer?

2. Who on your team works with the customer?

3. What programs have the client run in the past?

4. What have their spending levels been?

5. How have you serviced customers?

6. How would customers rate you?

7. What is important to the client?

8. Are you delivering what the client needs?

9. Any variation between expectation & delivery?

# CUSTOMER HISTORY

| | | | |
|---|---|---|---|
| *Date Prepared:* | **[date]** | *Advertiser:* | **[client name]** |

## Account Overview

*1. How long have we worked with customer? Who has supported on our team?*

*2. What programs has client run with us in the past? What have spend levels been?*

*3. How have we serviced customer? How would customer rate us?*

*4. What is important to the client?*

*5. Are we delivering what the client needs? How much variation between expectation & delivery?*

# Build Customer Map: Who Supports You? Who Does Not?

**Key Items to Track by Person**

1. Purchase Decision-Maker (Yes or No)

2. Influencer or Consultant (Yes or No)

3. Ally of Our Competitor (Yes or No)

4. Vocal about capability and the value we bring to their company?

5. Provides internal and competitive insights

6. Alerts and guides us through the political sensitivities and issues

7. Helps our company create a differentiated & winning Value Proposition(s)?

8. Solicits our point of view on issues that go beyond our offering

# CUSTOMER RELATIONSHIP MAP

## [ENTER NAME OF CUSTOMER]

| | CONTACT 1 | CONTACT 2 | CONTACT 3 | CONTACT 4 | CONTACT 5 |
|---|---|---|---|---|---|
| **5 PEOPLE WE NEED TO KNOW AND SPEND TIME WITH** | | | | | |
| RELATIONSHIP QUALIFICATION >> Enter #'s in Rows 22-26 to Change Color | ANTI-SPONSOR | DETRACTOR | NEUTRAL | SUPPORTER | PARTNER ALLY |
| Name / Title | | | | | |
| *NOTES* | | | | | |
| Activity(ies) They Like | | | | | |
| Unique Facts About Them | | | | | |
| Have Spent Time with Outside of Office (Yes or No) | | | | | |
| Influencer or Decision Maker | | | | | |
| Ally of Our Competitor (Yes or No) | | | | | |
| Vocal about the value we bring to their company | 2 | 4 | 6 | 6 | 8 |
| Provides internal and competitive insights that strengthens our sales efforts | 2 | 4 | 6 | 6 | 8 |
| Alerts and guides us through political sensitivities within their organization | 2 | 4 | 6 | 6 | 8 |
| Helps our company position a winning Value Proposition | 2 | 4 | 4 | 6 | 8 |
| Solicits our point of view beyond the specifics of our offering | 2 | 4 | 4 | 6 | 8 |
| **RELATIONSHIP SCORE** | 10 | 20 | 26 | 30 | 40 |

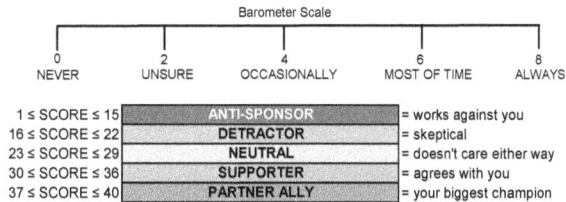

Barometer Scale

| 0 | 2 | 4 | 6 | 8 |
|---|---|---|---|---|
| NEVER | UNSURE | OCCASIONALLY | MOST OF TIME | ALWAYS |

| 1 ≤ SCORE ≤ 15 | ANTI-SPONSOR | = works against you |
|---|---|---|
| 16 ≤ SCORE ≤ 22 | DETRACTOR | = skeptical |
| 23 ≤ SCORE ≤ 29 | NEUTRAL | = doesn't care either way |
| 30 ≤ SCORE ≤ 36 | SUPPORTER | = agrees with you |
| 37 ≤ SCORE ≤ 40 | PARTNER ALLY | = your biggest champion |

# At The Meeting: Get Customers To Ask Questions & Engage

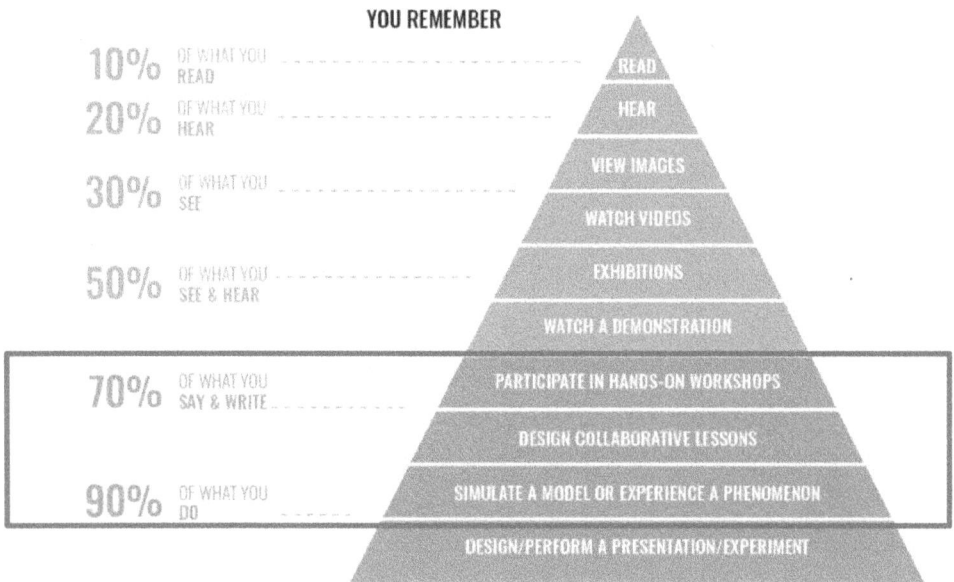

YOU REMEMBER

| | |
|---|---|
| **10%** OF WHAT YOU READ | READ |
| **20%** OF WHAT YOU HEAR | HEAR |
| **30%** OF WHAT YOU SEE | VIEW IMAGES |
| | WATCH VIDEOS |
| **50%** OF WHAT YOU SEE & HEAR | EXHIBITIONS |
| | WATCH A DEMONSTRATION |
| **70%** OF WHAT YOU SAY & WRITE | PARTICIPATE IN HANDS-ON WORKSHOPS |
| | DESIGN COLLABORATIVE LESSONS |
| **90%** OF WHAT YOU DO | SIMULATE A MODEL OR EXPERIENCE A PHENOMENON |
| | DESIGN/PERFORM A PRESENTATION/EXPERIMENT |

## EDGAR DALE "CONE OF EXPERIENCE"

# Meeting Follow-up – Become the Best at Follow-Up

- **Do same day as meeting, no exceptions!**

  - Recap goal(s) of meeting

  - List attendees at meeting

  - Keynotes from meeting

  - Next steps (And owner of each step)

- **Can just be in the body of an email**

  - But must be thorough

  - Showed you paid attention…

# Note -Taking

# – Brings Value to Others

- **Recap Goals of Meeting**

- Highlight 2 -3 key items covered


- **List Attendees**

- If a new contact, include their LinkedIn URL to

  show you took the extra time to learn about them


- **Notes**

- Scribble down key items on "paper", never type on

  laptop in meeting out of respect.


- **Next Steps**

- Have 3-5 next steps with an owner for each item

# Create a Project Tracker
## – Graphical or Linear

| Issues | Solutions | Dates | Messages |
|--------|-----------|-------|----------|
|  |  |  |  |
|  |  |  |  |
|  |  |  |  |
|  |  |  |  |
|  |  |  |  |
|  |  |  |  |

**ACTION ITEMS >**

**Innovation & Accountability *(Continuous Improvement)***

# Create a Project Tracker
## – Graphical or Linear

**NAME OF PROJECT + (OWNER)**

| Item/Milestone | Owner | % Done | Target Date | Week of >> January |
|---|---|---|---|---|
| | | | | |
| | | | | |
| | | | | |
| | | | | |
| | | | | |
| | | | | |
| | | | | |
| | | | | |
| | | | | |
| | | | | |
| | | | | |
| | | | | |
| | | | | |
| | | | | |
| | | | | |
| | | | | |
| | | | | |
| | | | | |
| | | | | |
| | | | | |
| | | | | |
| | | | | |
| | | | | |
| | | | | |
| | | | | |
| | | | | |
| | | | | |
| | | | | |

# LAUNCH TRACKER & TIMELINE

| February | March | April | May | June | July | August | September | October | November | December | Status/Next Steps |
|---|---|---|---|---|---|---|---|---|---|---|---|
| | | | | | | | | | | | |
| | | | | | | | | | | | |
| | | | | | | | | | | | |
| | | | | | | | | | | | |
| | | | | | | | | | | | |
| | | | | | | | | | | | |
| | | | | | | | | | | | |
| | | | | | | | | | | | |
| | | | | | | | | | | | |
| | | | | | | | | | | | |
| | | | | | | | | | | | |
| | | | | | | | | | | | |
| | | | | | | | | | | | |
| | | | | | | | | | | | |
| | | | | | | | | | | | |
| | | | | | | | | | | | |
| | | | | | | | | | | | |
| | | | | | | | | | | | |
| | | | | | | | | | | | |
| | | | | | | | | | | | |
| | | | | | | | | | | | |
| | | | | | | | | | | | |
| | | | | | | | | | | | |
| | | | | | | | | | | | |
| | | | | | | | | | | | |
| | | | | | | | | | | | |

The "NINE TOOL" to Inform Your Sales Process

# Remember... Customers Like Innovation & Improvement

**1. Conduct internal & external interviews**

**2. Chart out the buyer experience**

**3. List who is not buying you but should**

**4. Build a "S.W.O.T."**

(Strengths / Weaknesses / Opportunities / Threats)

- Internal > Strengths & weaknesses

- External > Threats and opportunities

**5. Think Through "4 Actions"**

- > Reduce, raise, eliminate and create

**6. "T.O.W.S." (S.W.O.T. Backwards, that's all...)**

- Uses SWOT to write out new strategies

**7. Create 8 slides internal deck on how / what you sell**

**8. Create 9 slide external customer presentation**

**9. Synthesize into a:10 and:30 second elevator pitch**

# First, Find Out What Others Depend on You For!

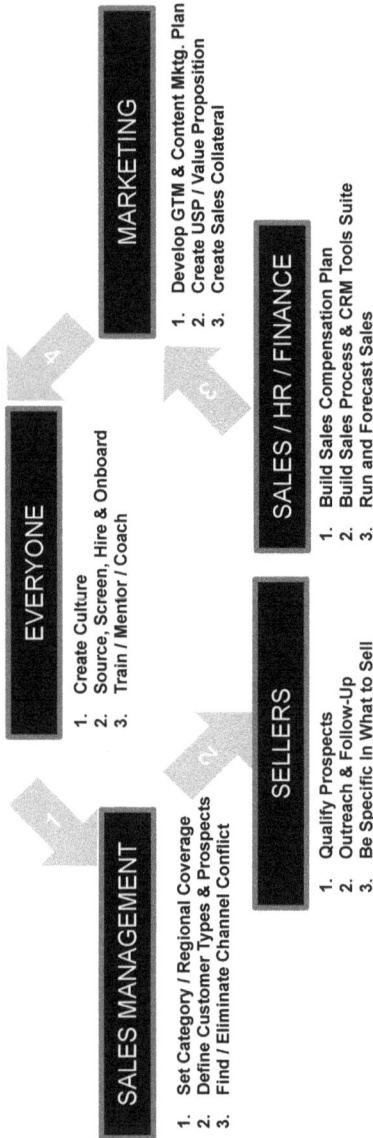

**MARKETING**
1. Develop GTM & Content Mktg. Plan
2. Create USP / Value Proposition
3. Create Sales Collateral

**SALES / HR / FINANCE**
1. Build Sales Compensation Plan
2. Build Sales Process & CRM Tools Suite
3. Run and Forecast Sales

**EVERYONE**
1. Create Culture
2. Source, Screen, Hire & Onboard
3. Train / Mentor / Coach

**SELLERS**
1. Qualify Prospects
2. Outreach & Follow-Up
3. Be Specific In What to Sell

**SALES MANAGEMENT**
1. Set Category / Regional Coverage
2. Define Customer Types & Prospects
3. Find / Eliminate Channel Conflict

**1**

### Positives/What Sellers Like at Our Company

| | | |
|---|---|---|
| | | |
| | | |
| | | |

**WHAT SELLERS LIKE AT YOUR COMPANY >**

### What Clients Like About Our Company'

| | | |
|---|---|---|
| | | |
| | | |
| | | |

**WHAT CLIENTS LIKE ABOUT YOUR COMPANY >**

# SELLER & CUSTOMER QUESTIONS

| Issues/What Sellers do NOT Like at Our Company | | |
|---|---|---|
| | | |
| | | |
| | | |

WHAT SELLERS

DO NOT LIKE

AT YOUR

< COMPANY

| What Clients do NOT Like About Our Company | | |
|---|---|---|
| | | |
| | | |
| | | |

WHAT CLIENTS

DO NOT LIKE

ABOUT YOUR

< COMPANY

**2**

[YOUR LOGO HERE]

**Uncovering blocks to buyer utility:**
Identify biggest problem areas/blocks

## The Six Stages of the

| | 1. Purchase | 2. Delivery | 3. Use |
|---|---|---|---|
| **a. What Stages Are Working Well** | | | |
| **b. What Stages Have Problems?** | | | |

How long does it take to hear back from a seller or CSM? Are proposals & IOs turned around quickly? Do sellers entertain customers prior to sale? Once bought how do you follow-up, invoices on time?

How long does it take to go live? How difficult is it to work with rep and senior team? Do buyers have to run reports themselves? If yes, how costly and difficult is this for buyer?

Does the product require training or expert assistance? How effective are the product's features and functions? Does the product or service deliver far more targeting or options than required by the average advertiser?

# BUYER UTILITY

* In which stage are the biggest blocks to customer productivity?
* In which stages are the biggest blocks to simplicity?
* In which stage are the biggest blocks to convenience?
* In which stage are the biggest blocks to reducing risks?
* In which stage are the biggest blocks to fun and image?

## Buyer Experience Cycle

| 4. Supplements | 5. Maintenance | 6. Upsell/Renew |
|---|---|---|
|  |  |  |
|  |  |  |

| Do you need other vendors to make this product work? If so, how costly are they? | How easy is it to maintain deal, and upgrade the buy? How costly is campaign maintenance? | What happens when campaign ends? How easy is it to wrap up and then move to renewal? |

**3**

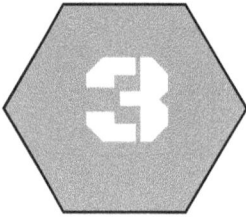

[YOUR LOGO HERE]

| What Companies Should Buy You, but Are Not? |
|---|

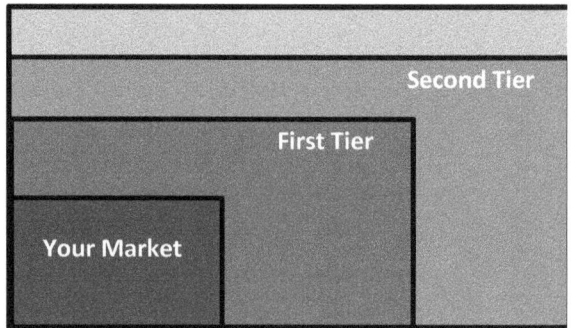

| First Tier Targets | Second |
|---|---|
| Target 1 | Target 1 |
| Target 2 | Target 2 |
| Target 3 | Target 3 |
| Target 4 | Target 4 |
| Target 5 | Target 5 |

# NON CUSTOMERS

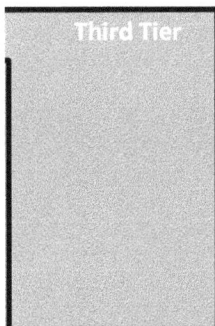

**Third Tier**

**First Tier**: Companies Ready to Try Your Product/Service

**Second Tier**: Companies That Have Said They Do Not Want Your Product/Service

**Third Tier:** Companies Outside of Your Typical Customer, Not in Your Industry, Would Never Know You Existed

**Tier Targets**

**Third Tier Targets**

Target 1

Target 2

Target 3

Target 4

Target 5

**4**

[YOUR LOGO HERE]

| | STRENGTHS |
|---|---|
| **INTERNAL** | 1) <br> 2) <br> 3) <br> 4) <br> 5) |

| | OPPORTUNITIES |
|---|---|
| **EXTERNAL** | 1) <br> 2) <br> 3) <br> 4) <br> 5) |

# S.W.O.T.

## WEAKNESSES

1)

2)

3)

4)

5)

## THREATS

1)

2)

3)

4)

5)

**5**

[YOUR LOGO HERE]

## Use this Exercise to Challenge

**List up to five factors for each (keep responses brief):**

### Reduce

Which factors should be *reduced below* industry's standard? (Think Costs)

1
2
3
4
5

### Eliminate

Which factors the industry takes for granted to elminate? (Think Costs)

1
2
3
4
5

### Summary of

# FOUR ACTION FRAMEWORK

## the Status Quo of Your Industry

### Raise

Which factors should be *raised above* industry's standard? (Think investment)

1
2
3
4
5

### Create

Which factors should be *created* that industry has never offered? (Think investment)

1
2
3
4
5

### Differentiation

| | Strengths (S) |
|---|---|
| **Internal Factors** | 1) |
| | 2) |
| What do you control internally? Where do you need to partner externally? What are the fastest wins? | 3) |
| **External Factors** | 4) |
| | 5) |
| **Opportunities (O)** | **SO Strategies** |
| 1) | 1 |
| 2) | |
| 3) | 2 |
| 4) | |
| 5) | 3 |
| **Threats (T)** | **ST Strategies** |
| 1) | 1 |
| 2) | |
| 3) | 2 |
| 4) | |
| 5) | 3 |

TOWS is simply SWOT spelled backwards: Strengths, Weaknesses, Opportunities, and Threats.

TOWS matrix is effective way to brainstorm specific strategies to address the results of SWOT investigation.

S-O strategies pursue opportunities that match the company's strengths.

W-O strategies overcome weaknesses to pursue opportunities.

# TOWS- NEW STRATEGIES

| Weaknesses (W) |
| --- |
| 1) |
| 2) |
| 3) |
| 4) |
| 5) |

| WO Strategies |
| --- |
| 1 |
| 2 |
| 3 |

| WT Strategies |
| --- |
| 1 |
| 2 |
| 3 |

**S-T** strategies identify ways you can use strengths to reduce vulnerability to external threats.

**W-T** strategies establish a defensive plan to prevent weaknesses from making you susceptible to external threats.

## 8 Slide Internal New Seller Company Education

| Overview | Customer | Type of Sale |
|---|---|---|
| What you do? | How many types of customers do you have? What categories by type? | Is this a complex sale or a short term / relatiionship driven sale? |
| | | |

| Alternatives | Value Points |
|---|---|
| Who else is doing this? What are customers alternatives | What are the differentiators vs. competitors? |
| | |

# INTERNAL MESSAGE

| Who is Seller? | Price/Fee |
|---|---|
| Direct sales, inside sales, Indirect/3rd party sales? | What is the price or fee you will charge? What do competitors charge? |
| | |

| Target Customer |
|---|
| What brands are you targeting? |
| |

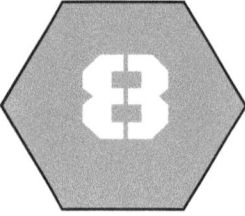

[YOUR LOGO HERE]

## 9 Slide External Seller to Customer Presentation

| Market | Problem You Solve | Product/Service |
|---|---|---|
| What part of advertising market are you creating value for? What are the key trends? | What problems do you have solutions for that talk to each client type? | What are your products & services? How do they work? |
| | | |

| Proof | Customer Benefits |
|---|---|
| What proof or evidence is there to substantiate your value proposition? | List Benefits for customer. How do you make the customers life better? |
| | |

# EXTERNAL MESSAGING

| Market Benefits | Alternatives |
|---|---|
| What are the benefits the market will derive from the product or service? | What alternative options does the market have to your product? How are you better? |
|  |  |

| Costs | Value Gained |
|---|---|
| List Costs for customer | List Value or ROI gained for customer. |
|  |  |

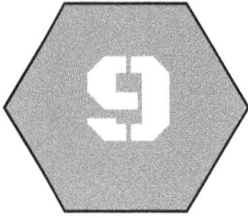

**[YOUR LOGO HERE]**

## 10 Second Sales Pitch

**Address what we do?**
The main job of our company is to...
•Item 1
•Item 2
•Item 3

**Address what makes us different?**
We are different because...
•Item 1
•Item 2
•Item 3

**Address how we're better?**
Other customers like that we offer...
•Item 1
•Item 2
•Item 3

# ELEVATOR MESSAGES

## 30 Second Sales Pitch

*Use 10 Sec pitch plus...*

**Recent news and awads**
Some highlights from the past few months...
•Item 1
•Item 2
•Item 3

**Address how customers can do X with us...**
Do X through...
•Item 1
•Item 2
•Item 3

**What is new with you and your company?**
Ask to get time on phone / Zoom / in Person to talk aobut...
•Item 1
•Item 2
•Item 3

# Create Customer Advisory Board

- 3 - 5 current clients that love your industry and will help you
  - All need to get approval to join and ok being in a launch press release

- Product surveys 1x / quarter

- Available for quick question/answer from time to time

- Annual dinner for all 3 -5 people

- Provide a special incentive that works for your company

# 07.

Forging Exceptionalism

# Mindset & Muscle Memory

**PLAN**     **TRAIN**     **VISUALIZE**

VISUALIZE HOW YOU WILL MAKE CONTACT

**VISUALIZE HOW YOU WILL FOLLOW-UP**

VISUALIZE SENDING THE PROPOSAL

**VISUALIZE GETTING TO AN AGREEMENT**

VISUALIZE GETTING PAID!

# Your Thoughts & Words Matter

- **What you think is what happens**
  - Think positively to end up in good situations
- **What you write down is where you go**
  - Like bowling, the direction of your thumb determines the direction of the ball
  - Get your thumb moving and write down your goals and plans
  - And use positive language!

# Avoid Anger & Keep Your Ego in Check

- At times we get upset...
  - When someone says or does something that offends us
  - When someone does not see the value we bring
- To eliminate ego...
  - Find value in others, compliment them, ask them how they are doing
  - Make others feel like an insider and valued, they will return this favor

# Failure, It is a Good System

- **Those that fail regularly are the ones that keep trying**
  - And... Better equipped to face the next challenge
- **Change up strategies and ask others for help**
  - Nothing is easy, we all make mistakes, but persevere
- **In the end, failure builds confidence!**

# No Surprises

- **Always keep others in the loop**
  - No one should find out key items by accident
- **Let people know what you are doing, before you do it**
- **Share the credit, own the faults**
  - Remove ego as often as you can

# Own The Effort!

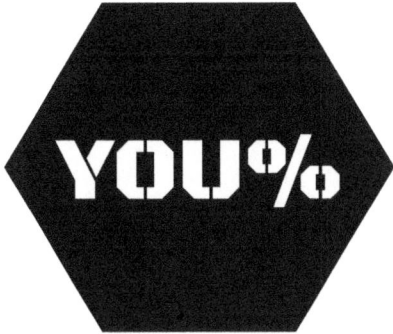

**YOU%**

**THEM%**

WHAT % OF EFFORT SHOULD YOU PUT IN?

**SHOULD ANOTHER PUT IN?**

# Lead by Example

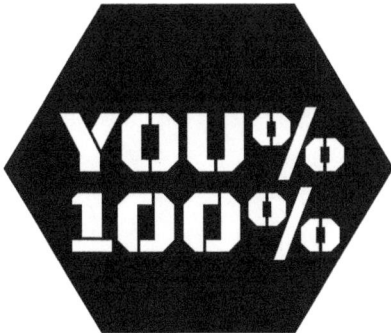

**YOU% 100%**

**THEM 0%**

**PUT IN THE WORK AND HAVE AN ANYTHING IS POSSIBLE, POSITIVE MINDSET**

# Maximizing
# Communication- LLTQC

LOOK / LISTEN / THINK / QUESTION / COMMUNICATE

# LOOK – What are the Non-Verbal Signals?

- **Pay attention to inconsistencies**
- Nonverbal communication should reinforce what is being said
- Is the person saying one thing, but their **body language conveying something else?**
- **Look at nonverbal communication signals as a group**
- Don't read too much into a single gesture or nonverbal cue

# Examples of Visual Inconsistencies

Look for clusters of behaviors and trust your gut!

- **Smile.** Real or fake?

- **Timing.** Fast, slow, or just right?

- **Voice.** Pitch changing, rambling?

- **Answers.** Answer questions or avoid?

- **Feet.** Shuffling or stretching

- **Face.** Cover nose, mouth, or eyes

- **Looking Away.** Look down and away, then glance back to see if you bought the falsehood

# LISTEN – Active Listening

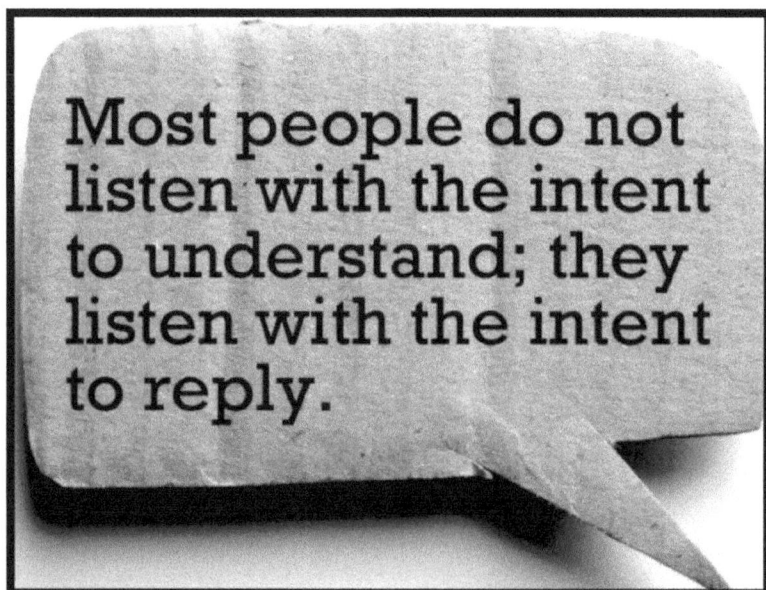

Most people do not listen with the intent to understand; they listen with the intent to reply.

# LOOK – What are the Non-Verbal Signals?

- Eye contact with the speaker

- Don't interrupt, and take notes if needed

- **Try not to plan what to say next**

- Show that you're listening, nod your head

- Ask simple, quick questions

- Paraphrase / Summarize

  - So, if heard correctly you said, XYZ

# THINK – Bring Together What You are Seeing & Hearing

- **Make maps**

- Mentally or on paper draw out to find which items depend on other items

- **Learn / Study**

- If you do not understand a word or topic, Google it...

- Or go to YouTube University

# QUESTION – Focus on What You Ask

- Be concise, ask one question at a time
- If you ask several questions at once some won't get answered
- **If you need a clock, speak for 20 seconds or less at a time**
- Take notes as needed...

# COMMUNICATE – Once You Have Your Input, Communicate

- Run through: Look, Listen, Think, and Question...
- While this has not stopped me from saying stupid stuff, it helps me focus before talking/communicating, most of the time
- Wait "3 Seconds" before you reply to anyone after they talk

# "85% OF YOUR FINANCIAL SUCCESS IS DUE TO PERSONALITY AND ABILITY TO COMMUNICATE, NEGOTIATE AND LEAD. ONLY 15% IS DUE TO TECHNICAL KNOWLEDGE."

## CARNEGIE INSTITUTE OF TECHNOLOGY

"SEVEN STEP PR" to Gain Inbound Leads & Drive Revenue

# PR = Public Relations & Press Releases – Do Both!

1. Highlight your company's basic info

2. Map out your content marketing program steps

3. Map out your public relations and press release efforts

4. Develop your primary, secondary & tertiary messages by audience

5. List out media outlets to contact by key category

6. List out names of reporters and contact info by a media outlet

7. Develop a list of events to attend & panels you want to speak on

# 1

# [YOUR LOGO HERE]

| BASIC INFO | DETAILS | COMPANY FOUNDATION |
|---|---|---|
| Company Name | | Company Mission |
| Company Spelling | | Why Work with FitAd |
| Company URL | | Company Vision |
| Company Tag Line | | What do we do? |
| When did company launch? | | What do we NOT do? |

# COMPANY INFO
## Fall 202X

| DETAILS | PR & MESSAGING | DETAILS |
|---|---|---|
| | **Key Messages for Core Audiences** | |
| | **Key Message for Investors** | |
| | **3rd Party References** | |
| | **What is our product?** | |
| | **What is unique about us?** | |

# 2

# [YOUR LOGO HERE]

## CONTENT MARKETING & FACE

| Items (In Priority Order, Focus On Low Cost, But Effective Items First) | KPI | Daily or Weekly |
|---|---|---|
| **SALES DRIVEN** | | |
| Client Meetings - General | | << x >> |
| Client Meetings - Breakfast / Lunch & Learns | | << x >> |
| Happy Hours & Dinners - 10-30 PPL | | |
| Conferences / Events -  2 Tickets to Attend | | |
| | | |
| **MARKETING DRIVEN** | | |
| PR / Reporter Outreach / Press Releases | | |
| Research Reports - Internal Data | | |
| Holiday Cards & Gifts | | |
| Newsletters to Customers & Prospects | | |
| Questionnaires to Customers & Prospects | | |
| White Papers on Key Topics | | |
| Research Reports - Third Party Driven | | |
| Conferences / Events -  Sponsorshp | | |
| | | |
| **SALES OUTBOUND COMM. FLOW** | | |
| Intro Note | | << x >> |
| Follow Up #1 | | << x >> |
| Follow Up #2 | | |
| Phone Call #1 | | |

# CONTENT MARKETING OVERVIEW
## Fall 202X

## TO FACE INTERACTION PLAN

| 2x / Month | 1x / Month | Quarterly |
| --- | --- | --- |
| | << x >> | |
| | | << x >> |
| | << x >> | |
| | | << x >> |
| | | << x >> |
| | << x >> | |
| | | << x >> |
| | | << x >> |
| | | << x >> |
| | | << x >> |
| << x >> | | |
| | << x >> | |

# WHY YOU NEED A CONTENT MARKETING PLAN

**BUYER JOURNEY**

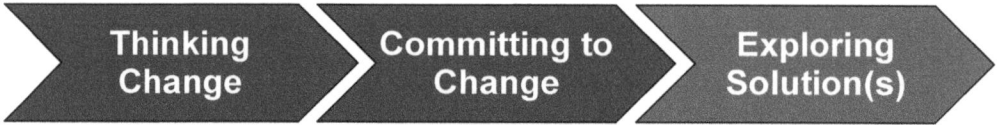

| Thinking Change | Committing to Change | Exploring Solution(s) |
|---|---|---|

**SELLER JOURNEY**

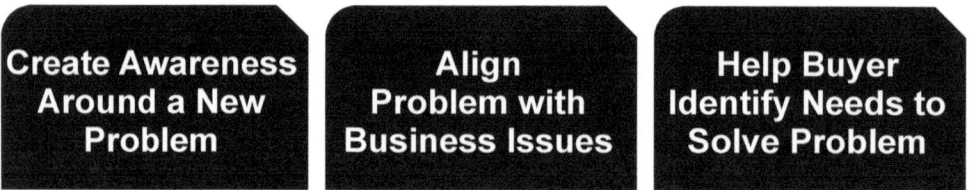

| Create Awareness Around a New Problem | Align Problem with Business Issues | Help Buyer Identify Needs to Solve Problem |
|---|---|---|

**SELLER DELIVERY OF CONTENT / PROOF TO BUYER**

| Research / White Papers | Webcasts / Events | Assessment Tools |
|---|---|---|

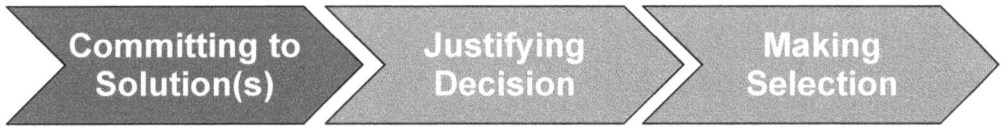

| Committing to Solution(s) | Justifying Decision | Making Selection |
|---|---|---|
| Align Solution W/ Specific Sets Of Bus. Needs | Make Business Case for Change | Validate / Reinforce Choice. Prove Best Value |
| Case Studies / Testimonials | ROI Analysis Tools | Feature Comparison |

# 3

**[YOUR LOGO HERE]**

| Week 1 | Week 2 | Week 3 | Week 4 | Week 5 | Week 6 |
|--------|--------|--------|--------|--------|--------|
| PRESS RELEASE #1 | | | | | |
| Kick-Off Call | Finalize media target list | Draft **FIRST** formal press release | Pitch announcement to business reporters | | Draft **SECOND** press release |
| Write Messaging Plan | Draft PR plan | Pitch announcement exclusive | Pitch announcement to tech reporters | | Finalize **SECOND** release |
| Audit background materials / media kits | Finalize PR plan | Create speaking calendar/matrix | Pitch announcement to ad/marketing reporters | Repeat Week #4 Until Enough Outlets Cover the Story | Draft thought leadership editorial calendar |
| v1 list of media outlets to target | Determine pitching strategy for **FIRST** announcement (exclusive?) | Finalize additional press targets for announcement release | Pitch announcement to general interest, as appropriate | | Finalize speaking calendar/matrix |
| | | Status update meeting | Pitch announcement to regional reporters | | Pitch speaking opps |
| | | Create interview schedule matrix | Status update meeting | | Status update meeting |
| | | Coordinate exclusive interview | Coordinate interviews | | |

# PR PLAN
## Fall 202X

| Week 7 | Week 8 | Week 9 | Week 10 | Week 11 | Week 12 |
|--------|--------|--------|---------|---------|---------|
| PRESS RELEASE #2 | | PRESS RELEASE #3 | | | NEXT WAVE PREP |
| Pitch **SECOND** press release to business reporters | | Draft **THIRD** press release | Pitch **THIRD** press release to business reporters | | Develop press release calendar for next three months |
| Pitch announcement to tech reporters | | Finalize **THIRD** press release | Pitch announcement to tech reporters | | |
| Pitch announcement to ad/marketing reporters | Repeat Week #7 Until Enough Outlets Cover the Story | Draft thought leadership editorial calendar | Pitch announcement to ad/marketing reporters | Repeat Week #10 Until Enough Outlets Cover the Story | |
| Pitch announcement to general interest, as appropriate | | Finalize speaking calendar/matrix | Pitch announcement to general interest, as appropriate | | |
| Pitch announcement to regional reporters | | Pitch speaking opps | Pitch announcement to regional reporters | | |
| Status update meeting | | Status update meeting | Status update meeting | | |
| Coordinate interviews | | | Coordinate interviews | | |

# 4

# [YOUR LOGO HERE]

| | Why Company matters | Primary Message |
|---|---|---|
| **Everyone** | | |

| | Why Company matters | Primary Message |
|---|---|---|
| **Audience 1** | | |

| | Why Company matters | Primary Message |
|---|---|---|
| **Audience 2** | | |

| | Why Company matters | Primary Message |
|---|---|---|
| **Audience 3** | | |

| | Why Company matters | Primary Message |
|---|---|---|
| **Audience 4** | | |

| | Why Company matters | Primary Message |
|---|---|---|
| **Investors** | | |

# MESSAGING
## Fall 202X

**Secondary Message**     **Tertiary Message**

**Secondary Message**     **Tertiary Message**

**Secondary Message**     **Tertiary Message**

**Secondary Message**     **Tertiary Message**

**Secondary Message**     **Tertiary Message**

**Secondary Message**     **Tertiary Message**

# [YOUR LOGO HERE]

| General Interest | Business | Media |
| --- | --- | --- |

# MEDIA OUTLETS
## Fall 202X

| Advertising | National | Regional | Local |
| --- | --- | --- | --- |

**6**

# [YOUR LOGO HERE]

| Name | Outlet | Comment | Email |
|------|--------|---------|-------|

# KEY REPORTER LIST
## Fall 202X

| Twitter | Articles Link |
| --- | --- |

**7**

# [YOUR LOGO HERE]    EVENT

| Name | Outlet | Comment | Email |
|------|--------|---------|-------|
|      |        |         |       |

# & PANEL OPPORTUNITIES
## Fall 202X

| Twitter | Event Link |
| --- | --- |

# Once Your Story Is Locked, Use "PR" To Promote

- Public relations to push your press release is essential

- Drives inbound leads

- Provides buyers with proof

- Makes it easier to earn meetings

- Helps earn panel & keynote opportunities

- Make it easier to hire PR & marketing firms once ready

Personal & Team
Development Tools

# DAILY - Personal Battle Boards (Two Examples)

*BATTLE BOARD*

**[YOUR LOGO HERE]**

PLAY LIKE A CHAMPION / FIRST TO GET ANGRY LOSES / I DO WHAT OTHERS WON'T / I VISUALIZE SUCCESS / WRITE DOWN THE PLAN / COMMUNICATE THE PLAN / TAKE THE NEXT STEP / ACTION, OVER IDEAS / QUESTION ANYTHING / IMPROVE EVERYTHING / I TALK LESS / I DO MORE.

**TODAY**
1
2
3

**THIS WEEK**
1
2
3
4
5
6
7
8

**BUSINESS #1**
1 – 24

**BUSINESS #2**
1 – 24

**HR / STAFFING / ADMIN**
A A A A B B B B C C C C

**MARKETING / RESEARCH / EVENTS**
1
2
3
4
5
6

**TECH / INFRASTRUCTURE**
A A A B B C

**BUSINESS #3**
1 – 24

**PERSONAL GROWTH (IDEAS / BOOKS)**
1
2
3
4
5
6

**SALES MINDSET**
1 Be Nice. New Biz Daily. Bring Solutions.
2 5 / 5 / 30
3 6 Months Out Selling. ABM & Marketing
4 Legacy clients move to Act. Mngt.
5 Annuals, Upfronts, Advisory Board

**BUSINESS #4**
1 – 24

# BATTLE BOARD

[YOUR LOGO HERE]

PLAY LIKE A CHAMPION / FIRST TO GET ANGRY LOSES / DO WHAT OTHERS WON'T / VISUALIZE SUCCESS / WRITE DOWN THE PLAN / COMMUNICATE THE PLAN / TAKE THE NEXT STEP / ACTION OVER IDEAS / QUESTION ANYTHING / IMPROVE EVERYTHING / TALK LESS / DO MORE

## TODAY
1
2
3

## THIS WEEK
1
2
3
4
5
6
7
8

## BUSINESS #1
1
2
3
4
5
6
7
8
9
10
11

## BUSINESS #2
1
2
3
4
5
6
7
8
9
10
11
12

## HR / STAFFING / ADMIN
A
A
A
A
B
B
B
B
C
C
C
C

## BUSINESS #3
1
2
3
4
5
6
7
8
9
10
11

## BUSINESS #4
1
2
3
4
5
6
7
8
9
10
11
12

## MARKETING / RESEARCH / EVENTS
1
2
3
4
5
6

## TECH / INFRASTRUCTURE
A
A
A
B
B
C

## PERSONAL GROWTH (IDEAS / BOOKS)
1
2
3
4
5
6

## SALES MINDSET
1  Be Nice. New Biz Daily. Bring Solutions.
2  5 / 5 / 30
3  6 Months Out Selling, ABM & Marketing
4  Legacy clients move to Act. Mngt.
5  Annuals, Upfronts, Advisory Board

| PRIORITY #1 | PRIORITY #4 |
|---|---|
| PRIORITY #2 | PRIORITY #5 |
| PRIORITY #3 | PRIORITY #6 |

# WEEKLY – Quick Report (Even if Only for Personal Use)

**One Page Weekly Report**

1. Top 5 items completed this week

2. Top 5 items to focus on next week

3. Top risks and needs

4. Top prospects & follow-ups

5. Upcoming meetings, events

6. Top deals about to close

7. Top deals closed

# [NAME OF SELLER] WEEKLY REPORT

## TOP 5 ITEMS ACCOMPLISHED THIS WEEK

1)
2)
3)
4)
5)

## TOP 5 ITEMS FOR NEXT WEEK

1)
2)
3)
4)
5)

## TOP NEEDS

1)
2)
3)

## TOP RISKS

1)
2)
3)

| MONDAY | TUESDAY | WEDNESDAY | THURSDAY | FRIDAY |
|--------|---------|-----------|----------|--------|

**TOP 5 DAILY PROSPECTS**

**TOP 5 DAILY FOLLOW-UPS**

**MEETINGS & EVENTS**

## UPCOMING MEETINGS

1)
2)
3)
4)
5)

## UPCOMING EVENTS / CONFERNECES

1)

**PIPELINE & DEAL SNAPSHOT**

## TOP 5 DEALS WORKING TO CLOSE

1)
2)
3)
4)
5)

## TOP 5 MOST RECENT DEALS CLOSED

1)

9. BLANK WEEKLY REPORT | WEEK NUMBER

# QUARTERLY – Sales Velocity Calculator (Use Before New Q)

1. Focus on getting the right prospects, not just any prospects

2. Increase avg. deal value/size

3. Increase win rate %

4. Reduce the time needed to close each deal

# SALES VELOCITY

## KEY = Update Five Light Gray Cells ONLY

| | # of Deals | x | Average Deal Size | x | % Win Rate |
| --- | --- | --- | --- | --- | --- |
| | | | Length of Sales Cycle (Months) | | |

**Current Sales Velolcity**

| # of Deals in Pipeline | Avg, Deal Size | % Win Rate | Velocity | % Improvement |
| --- | --- | --- | --- | --- |
| 30 | $ 50,000 | 50% | $ 375,000 | 48% |
| | 2 | | | |

Length of Sales Cycle (Months)

**New Sales Velocity**

| | | | | |
| --- | --- | --- | --- | --- |
| 10% | | | | |
| 33 | $ 55,000 | 55% | $ 554,583 | |
| | 1.8 | | | |

$179,00 IMPROVEMENT

**Notes:**
1) Focus time on getting the right prospects, not just any prospects
2) Then focus on increasing avg. deal value, win rate and at same time reduce your sales cycle to closure

# QUARTERLY
# Seller Scorecard

**[YOUR LOGO HERE]**

| Quarter | Measure | Notes |
|---------|---------|-------|
| **Q1** | Sales Revenue (Performance)<br># Pipeline Deals (Effectiveness)<br># of New Outbounds (Effectiveness)<br>Biz Dev (Effectiveness)<br>**Performance** (10 = Score Goal)<br>**Effectiveness** (10 = Score Goal) | Individual Goal<br>Maintain 30 Deals / Each Day<br>5 New Outbounds / Day - 300 / Quarter<br>5 Follow - Ups / Day - 300 / Quarter |
| **Q2** | Sales Revenue (Performance)<br># Pipeline Deals (Effectiveness)<br># of New Outbounds (Effectiveness)<br>Biz Dev (Effectiveness)<br>**Performance** (10 = Score Goal)<br>**Effectiveness** (10 = Score Goal) | Individual Goal<br>Maintain 30 Deals / Each Day<br>5 New Outbounds / Day - 300 / Quarter<br>5 Follow - Ups / Day - 300 / Quarter |
| **Q3** | Sales Revenue (Performance)<br># Pipeline Deals (Effectiveness)<br># of New Outbounds (Effectiveness)<br>Biz Dev (Effectiveness)<br>**Performance** (10 = Score Goal)<br>**Effectiveness** (10 = Score Goal) | Individual Goal<br>Maintain 30 Deals / Each Day<br>5 New Outbounds / Day - 300 / Quarter<br>5 Follow - Ups / Day - 300 / Quarter |
| **Q4** | Sales Revenue (Performance)<br># Pipeline Deals (Effectiveness)<br># of New Outbounds (Effectiveness)<br>Biz Dev (Effectiveness)<br>**Performance** (10 = Score Goal)<br>**Effectiveness** (10 = Score Goal) | Individual Goal<br>Maintain 30 Deals / Each Day<br>5 New Outbounds / Day - 300 / Quarter<br>5 Follow - Ups / Day - 300 / Quarter |

# FY 20XX SELLER SCORECARD
## <NAME OF SALESPERSON>

| Goal | Actual | Result | Weight | Q1 Score |
|---|---|---|---|---|
| $450,000 | $500,000 | 111% | 1.00 | 11.11 |
| 30 | 25 | 83% | 0.60 | 5.00 |
| 300 | 100 | 33% | 0.20 | 0.67 |
| 300 | 100 | 33% | 0.20 | 0.67 |
| | | | | **10.0** |
| | | | | **6.3** |
| $450,000 | $500,000 | 111% | 1.00 | 11.11 |
| 30 | 25 | 83% | 0.60 | 5.00 |
| 300 | 100 | 33% | 0.20 | 0.67 |
| 300 | 100 | 33% | 0.20 | 0.67 |
| | | | | **10.0** |
| | | | | **6.3** |
| $450,000 | $500,000 | 111% | 1.00 | 11.11 |
| 30 | 25 | 83% | 0.60 | 5.00 |
| 300 | 100 | 33% | 0.20 | 0.67 |
| 300 | 100 | 33% | 0.20 | 0.67 |
| | | | | **10.0** |
| | | | | **6.3** |
| $450,000 | $500,000 | 111% | 1.00 | 11.11 |
| 30 | 25 | 83% | 0.60 | 5.00 |
| 300 | 100 | 33% | 0.20 | 0.67 |
| 300 | 100 | 33% | 0.20 | 0.67 |
| | | | | **10.0** |
| | | | | **6.3** |

# QUARTERLY
# If You Have Budget for Paid Media – Use it!

**DIGITAL MARKETING PLAN**
FALL 202X

To create more than one line of text within a cell, simply hold down 'Alt' while you press 'Return'. If you're using a PC or for a Mac press 'Ctrl', 'Alt' and 'Return'

| | January | February | March | April | May | June | July | August | September | October | November | December |
|---|---|---|---|---|---|---|---|---|---|---|---|---|
| Your Key Campaigns or Events | Edit your key Campaigns and / or your own structure | | | | | | | | | | | |
| Any Special Offers & Sales Promotions | Add your offers and promotions | | | | | | | | | | | |

| DIGITAL MKTG. | January | February | March | April | May | June | July | August | September | October | November | December |
|---|---|---|---|---|---|---|---|---|---|---|---|---|
| Website | Short desc. of planned mktg | | | | | | | | | | | |
| Blogs | | | | | | | | | | | | |
| SEO / SEM | | | | | | | | | | | | |
| Email newsletters | | | | | | | | | | | | |
| Google AdWords | | | | | | | | | | | | |
| Geographical advertising (e.g. Google Places) | | | | | | | | | | | | |
| Affiliate marketing | | | | | | | | | | | | |
| Online business directories & findings | | | | | | | | | | | | |
| Facebook | | | | | | | | | | | | |
| Twitter | | | | | | | | | | | | |
| YouTube | | | | | | | | | | | | |
| Linkedin | | | | | | | | | | | | |
| Instagram | | | | | | | | | | | | |
| TikTok | | | | | | | | | | | | |
| Online press releases | | | | | | | | | | | | |
| Online reputation management | | | | | | | | | | | | |
| Mobile Apps (iPhone / Android) | | | | | | | | | | | | |
| Text / SMS | | | | | | | | | | | | |
| Bluetooth location-based marketing | | | | | | | | | | | | |
| Augmented reality | | | | | | | | | | | | |

**OFFLINE MARKETING PLAN**
FALL 202X

To create more than one line of text within a cell, simply hold down 'Alt' while you press 'Return'. If you're using a PC or for a Mac press 'Ctrl', 'Alt' and 'Return'

| | January | February | March | April | May | June | July | August | September | October | November | December |
|---|---|---|---|---|---|---|---|---|---|---|---|---|
| Your Key Campaigns or Events | Edit your key Campaigns and / or your own structure | | | | | | | | | | | |
| Any Special Offers & Store Promotions | Add your offers | | | | | | | | | | | |

| OFFLINE MKTG. | January | February | March | April | May | June | July | August | September | October | November | December |
|---|---|---|---|---|---|---|---|---|---|---|---|---|
| Direct mail | Short desc. of planned mktg | | | | | | | | | | | |
| Print advertising | | | | | | | | | | | | |
| Broadcast advertising | | | | | | | | | | | | |
| OOH - Events - Locations | | | | | | | | | | | | |
| Merchandising & point of sale | | | | | | | | | | | | |
| Personal selling | | | | | | | | | | | | |
| Telemarketing | | | | | | | | | | | | |
| Networking | | | | | | | | | | | | |
| Referrals | | | | | | | | | | | | |
| Case studies / Testimonials | | | | | | | | | | | | |
| Awards | | | | | | | | | | | | |
| Trade shows & exhibitions | | | | | | | | | | | | |
| Corporate events | | | | | | | | | | | | |
| Other events | | | | | | | | | | | | |
| Endorsements | | | | | | | | | | | | |
| Sponsorship | | | | | | | | | | | | |
| Interviews / Media presence | | | | | | | | | | | | |
| Speeches & presentations | | | | | | | | | | | | |
| Articles for publication | | | | | | | | | | | | |
| Press releases / News | | | | | | | | | | | | |
| Public relations & publicity | | | | | | | | | | | | |

[YOUR LOGO HERE]

## MARKETING BUDGET FOR DGTL & OFFLINE
FALL 202X

| DIGITAL MKTG. | January | February | March | April | May | June | July | August | September | October | November | December | YEARLY TOTAL |
|---|---|---|---|---|---|---|---|---|---|---|---|---|---|
| Website | | | | | | | | | | | | | |
| Blogs | | | | | | | | | | | | | |
| SEO / SEM | | | | | | | | | | | | | |
| Email newsletters | | | | | | | | | | | | | |
| Google AdWords | | | | | | | | | | | | | |
| Geographical advertising (e.g. Google Places) | | | | | | | | | | | | | |
| Affiliate marketing | | | | | | | | | | | | | |
| Facebook | | | | | | | | | | | | | |
| Twitter | | | | | | | | | | | | | |
| YouTube | | | | | | | | | | | | | |
| LinkedIn | | | | | | | | | | | | | |
| Instagram | | | | | | | | | | | | | |
| TikTok | | | | | | | | | | | | | |
| Online press releases | | | | | | | | | | | | | |
| Online reputation management | | | | | | | | | | | | | |
| Mobile Apps (iPhone / Android) | | | | | | | | | | | | | |
| Text / SMS | | | | | | | | | | | | | |
| Bluetooth location-based marketing | | | | | | | | | | | | | |
| Augmented reality | | | | | | | | | | | | | |
| ONLINE SUB-TOTAL | | | | | | | | | | | | | |

| OFFLINE MKTG. | January | February | March | April | May | June | July | August | September | October | November | December | YEARLY TOTAL |
|---|---|---|---|---|---|---|---|---|---|---|---|---|---|
| Direct mail | | | | | | | | | | | | | |
| Print advertising | | | | | | | | | | | | | |
| Broadcast advertising | | | | | | | | | | | | | |
| OOH - Events - Locations | | | | | | | | | | | | | |
| Merchandising & point of sale | | | | | | | | | | | | | |
| Telemarketing | | | | | | | | | | | | | |
| Networking | | | | | | | | | | | | | |
| Case studies / Testimonials | | | | | | | | | | | | | |
| Awards | | | | | | | | | | | | | |
| Trade shows & exhibitions | | | | | | | | | | | | | |
| Corporate events | | | | | | | | | | | | | |
| Endorsements | | | | | | | | | | | | | |
| Sponsorship | | | | | | | | | | | | | |
| Interviews / Media presence | | | | | | | | | | | | | |
| Speeches & presentations | | | | | | | | | | | | | |
| Articles for publication | | | | | | | | | | | | | |
| Press releases / News | | | | | | | | | | | | | |
| Public relations & publicity | | | | | | | | | | | | | |
| The personal touch (e.g. cards & gifts) | | | | | | | | | | | | | |
| OFFLINE SUB-TOTAL | | | | | | | | | | | | | |
| TOTAL (ONLINE & OFFLINE) | | | | | | | | | | | | | |

# SEMI ANNUALLY – SELF REVIEW

## Name: <Name>

**Are the expectations for your position clear ? Any items to call out?**

<Enter Your Info Here>

**What accomplishment(s) are you most proud of during 20xx?**

<Enter Your Info Here>

# Date of Review:    x/x/20xx

**What areas do you feel you need to improve upon to beat your 20xx goals?**

<Enter Your Info Here>

**What training or assistance would you like?**

<Enter Your Info Here>

# SEMI ANNUALLY –
# MANAGER REVIEW

| | | | % To Individual Sales Goal | |
|---|---|---|---|---|
| **Name:** | <Name> | | Q1 | **88%** |
| Title: | <Title> | | Q2 | **90%** |
| Today's Date: | 12/15/2022 | | Q3 | **95%** |
| Date of Hire: | 2/1/2018 | | Q4 | **107%** |
| Years in Position: | 4.87 | | 20xx | **95%** |
| Date of Review | 8/22/2022 | | | |

**DRIVE & FOCUS**

| | |
|---|---|
| Self Motivated | 4 |
| Positive Attitude | 4 |
| Go Above and Beyond Role | 3 |
| Attention to Detail | 3 |
| *SECTION RATING* | *3.5* |

**SALES PROCESS**

| | |
|---|---|
| Comfort Describing All of our Products | 3 |
| Can Easily Develop Sponsorship Ideas | 3 |
| Hits or Beats Quarterly Revenue Goals | 1 |
| 30+ Deals Always in Pipeline | 3 |
| Earn Premium Rates and CPMs | 4 |
| CRM Knowledge & Ability | 3 |
| Utilize CRM for All Deal / Campaign Activiy | 3 |
| *SECTION RATING* | *2.9* |

**LEADERSHIP SKILLS**

| | |
|---|---|
| Stays Calm in Conflict | 4 |
| Comfortable Asking for Help | 4 |
| Comfortable Delegating | 4 |
| Comfortable Managing Up | 4 |
| Develops Plans to Hit or Beat Sales Goals | 2 |
| Team Player / Positive Influence | 3 |
| *SECTION RATING* | *3.5* |

**EXTERNAL COMMUNICATION**

| | |
|---|---|
| Comfortable Telling Company Story | 3 |
| Comfortable Cold Calling | 3 |
| Regularly Builds Custom Decks for Pitches | 3 |
| Emails Short and Easily Understandable | 3 |
| Completes 5 New Business Outbounds / Day | 3 |
| *SECTION RATING* | *3.0* |

**INTERNAL COMMUNICATION**

| | |
|---|---|
| Readily Works with Support Teams | 3 |
| Communicates with other Reps on Deals | 3 |
| Follows Process to get Deals Done | 3 |
| *SECTION RATING* | *3.0* |

| **RANKING DEFINITIONS** |
|---|
| 5 = Consistently Exceeds Expectations |
| 4 = Exceeds Expectations |
| 3 = Achieves Expectations |
| 2 = Meets Some Expectations |
| 1 = Does Not Meet Expectations |

| *OVERALL RATING* | *3.2* |
|---|---|

**Manager Comments:**

# SECTION

# 11.

## If There is a Revenue Gap Find it. Fix it.

# Where is the Problem? What Are Your Best Practices?

- **Not about effort, just results**

- Although you do need LOTS of effort

- **Identify the problem**

- Three areas to investigate:

- 1) Product, 2) Marketplace Perception, or 3) Sellers

- **But... Even a bad seller can sell a great product**

- Typically lack of revenue is traced back to a lack of marketplace perception or poor sales goal planning

- **What is the best practice?**

- Create a best practice and get everyone on board

- **Aggression & innovation wins. Period.**

# Don't Wait For Clients To Show You The Problem

- ALWAYS know what is important to each client
- Understand if you are delivering what the client needs
- Determine the variation between expectation & delivery
- Become consistent & predictable in what the client sees from you

# Recap Of Key Items To Drive Revenue

## 1 - Prospecting

### a. Work in Units of "5"
AM - Outbound
PM - Follow-Up

### b. Outbound -> Customized
Create templates to speed process
NO email blasts, only 1:1 emails
Create your "Customer Journey"

### c. FIND Customer Problem(s) to Solve
Problems always changing, be in tune

**Tools**: ZoomInfo, Hunter, Winmo, RocketReach, InfoGroup... Outbound.io, ProspectIQ, Yesware, Tout....

## 2 - Content Mktg. / PR - Events

### a. Monthly Newsletters

Develop calendar to tie topics to annual
events and seasonalities for your industry

### b. Case Studies / Best Practices

Potentially hire a freelancer

### c. Thought Leadership / Industry Update

Find a topic or two to stand behind and
become the voice and leader in your space
send out updates each quarter or month.
Run surveys, 3-5 questions

**Tools**: Salesforce, MailChimp, Marketo, SurveyMonkey

## 3 - Goal Setting / Tracking

### a. Set Daily Goals

What to focus on and do each day

### b. Re-focus Weekly

Weekly report: Completed this week,
Focus for next week, Risk, and Needs

### c. Leverage CRM / Excel Tracker

Use for workflow management,
document storage.

**Tools**: Salesforce, Dropbox, Google Drive

Additional Resources to
Improve Your Revenue

# Your Health! No One Else Is Going To Do This For You...

- Drink water and Exercise

- Meditate or Learn to Meditate

- Read / Classes– Always improve

- Become Financially Literate

- Take Vacation and Travel

- The better shape you are in the more you can work

- The more you work the more others will take notice of you

- When people can count on you to always do more you will get promoted and make more money!

## PRIORITIZE MENTAL, PHYSICAL & FINANCIAL HEALTH

# Be Relentless!

- **Relentless Preparation**
  - Customer Brief & History


- **Relentless Outreach**
  - Daily 5's
  - Prospect in AM, Follow-Up in PM


- **Relentless Tracking**
  - Customer Mapping
  - Identify helpers and work to switch detractors


- **Always Take the Extra Step**


- **Do More Than Everyone Else**

## Minimum Daily Activity – The 5's

**5+ OUTBOUNDS BEFORE LUNCH**

**5+ FOLLOW-UPS BEFORE DINNER**

# Did This Book Deliver on the Three Benefits?

**01.**

Access New Tools To Grow Your Revenue Mindset

**02.**

Evolve Your Sales Process To Prioritize Prospecting & Follow-up

**03.**

Integrate Relentless Preparation Into Your Routine

# DGTLCORE.COM/SURVEY

# AUTHOR PROFILE

For the past 25 years Mort Greenberg has been a salesperson and sales manager for technology start-ups and larger media companies. These companies have included a variety of fund raising efforts, larger and small, to IPOs, and several mergers and acquisitions. Fighting his way up from an Account Executive to a role as a division President with 800+ employees, including 103 sellers delivering $220 million of annual revenue, you can guess there were many challenges that needed to be overcome. From the early Internet days at Excite.com he was fortunate to be part of a team that sold 5% of all ad revenue on the Internet in 1996 ($13M of $268M). He was among some of the first to create the marketplace for digital advertising. Being part of a small group tasked with rebuilding the revenue efforts for the search engine Ask Jeeves was a highlight for him and the group he worked with, right through its acquisition for $1.9 billion five years later. Learning lessons of the need for speed in decision making came from his time with Tel Aviv based Metacafe at the start of the Online video industry.

Much of his career has been about finding ways to be creative and do more with less resources. While at organizations like IAC InterActiveCorp, NBC Universal, Nokia and iHeartMedia he spent time developing systems to simplify go to market strategies. During his Nokia days he traveled the globe and learned from some of the most talented coworkers you could find in Brazil, Argentina, Mexico, England, Finland, Germany, UAE, India, Singapore and more. Along the way he launched two of his own companies, FitAd and MindFlight, and learned the hard way that start-ups are not always successful. For the past six years his time has been spent with a private equity firm to improve and grow 18 media properties in the military, defense, history and home and garden categories. The #1 lesson he has learned in the past few years is that by improving people's revenue mindset, business problems are healed and teams motivated through innovation that new revenue affords.

You can find me on most social media including LinkedIn and Twitter @MortGreenberg

# REVENUE.
# MINDSET.

www.ingramcontent.com/pod-product-compliance
Lightning Source LLC
Chambersburg PA
CBHW040926210326
41597CB00030B/5195